Blitzkrieg in the West, 1939–1942

Schwartze or 'black men' — the nickname given to *Luftwaffe* ground crew from the colour of their overalls — fit a crewman of a Me 110C of *Zerstörergeschwader* (Destroyer Wing) 76 with a parachute prior to a mission over Poland, September 1939. The twin engine fighter did extremely well in combat all the way through the fall of France, leading to complacency amongst 110 unit commanders.

LUFTWAFFE AT WAR

Blitzkrieg in the West, 1939–1942

Jeffrey L. Ethell

Greenhill Books
LONDON

Stackpole Books
PENNSYLVANIA

Greenhill Books

Jeffrey Lance Ethell. 29 September 1947 – 6 June 1997.

Blitzkrieg in the West, 1939-1942
first published 1997
by Greenhill Books, Lionel Leventhal Limited,
Park House, 1 Russell Gardens,
London NW11 9NN
and
Stackpole Books, 5067 Ritter Road, Mechanicsburg,
PA 17055, USA

British Library Cataloguing in Publication Data

Ethell, Jeffrey
Blitzkrieg in the West, 1939-1945. (Luftwaffe at war;
v. 3) 1. Germany, Luftwaffe 2. World War, 1939-1945
– Campaigns Western Front
I. Title
940.5'421
ISBN 1-85367-283-1

Library of Congress Cataloging-in-Publication Data

Ethell, Jeffrey L.
Blitzkrieg in the west. 1939-1942/Jeffrey L. Ethell.
72p. 26cm. – (Luftwaffe at war; v. 3)
ISBN 1-85367-283-1 (pbk.)
1. World War, 1939–1945 – Aerial operations, German. 2. Bombardment – Europe. 3. Germany. Luftwaffe – History – World War, 1939–45. 4. World War,
1939–1945 – Campaigns – Western Front. I. Title.
II. Series.
D787.E85 1997   97-20788
940.54'4943 – DC21   CIP

Designed by DAG Publications Ltd
Designed by David Gibbons.
Layout by Anthony A. Evans.
Edited by Ian Heath.
Printed and bound in Singapore.

BLITZKRIEG IN THE WEST, 1939–1942

When Germany invaded Poland on 1 September 1939, the pointed end of its mighty spear was the formidable *Luftwaffe*. Born from the ashes of Germany's ignominious defeat in the First World War, this potent force had been forged in secret and armed with the best that industry could provide. Former 'Richthofen's Flying Circus' ace Hermann Göring, one of Adolf Hitler's closest confidants, was put in command with virtually unlimited authority.

During the first year of the war the *Luftwaffe* proved to be just as deadly as the propagandists said. A superb tactical air force, it helped move the *Wehrmacht* and its Panzers from Poland through the Low Countries and into France. Its pilots, led by Spanish Civil War veterans who had revolutionised modern air combat, were far more experienced than their Allied counterparts, and had racked up prestigious quantities of air and ground victories by the time the French coast was reached.

With an invasion of England foremost in Hitler's mind, Göring boasted he could bring the island nation to its knees with the *Luftwaffe* alone during the summer of 1940. However, within a few months the strategic and doctrinal shortcomings of the mighty German air force had been exposed by a small band of British fighter pilots, significantly aided by scientific and industrial genius. By 1942 the inexorable German advance had ground to a halt everywhere. Hitler continued to order offensive operations, but the verve was gone.

This book traces that heady period of German success through the pictures of *Luftwaffe* personnel — pilots, crewmen and press photographers — who thought to preserve it on film. What quickly becomes evident is the aura of confidence and near invincibility that was instilled into those who served on the front line. The *Luftwaffe* was the first air force to prove the potential — and reveal the limits — of air power.

Author's note: For years controversy has raged regarding what prefix should be used when describing Messerschmitt aircraft — Bf or Me? Wartime German documents use both, though the Me prefix predominates. The following explanation is provided by Dr Winfried Heinemann of the Militärgeschictliches Forschungsamt, Potsdam: 'In 1927, Professor Willy Messerschmitt began a co-operation with the Bayerische Flugzeugwerke AG. He increased his share in the business during and after the Great Depression, until, in September 1938, the entire firm was renamed "Messerschmitt AG". Any aircraft designed before that time were officially designated as "Bf". This applies to the Bf 108 "Taifun" — even those models built after the Second World War — and also the Bf 109A-D series, whereas the E-Z versions bore the designator "Me". Similarly, the Bf 110A and B bore the former prefix, whereas the Me 110C-G bore the latter.' I have long subscribed to this convention, and follow it here.

The birth of the *Luftwaffe*

With the Paris Air Agreement of 1926, the last post-First World War restrictions (already very lenient) placed on civil aviation in the defeated countries were dropped. Germany had seized the opportunity to revive its aircraft industry by rushing headlong into the development of new aircraft, airlines, pilot training schemes, and glider clubs, in effect doing everything it could to regain its once-formidable lead in aviation technology. Behind all this activity was a small group of military officers, led by General Hans von Seeckt, who were determined to create a new air force in flagrant violation of the Treaty of Versailles.

Drawing the majority of his military air crews from Lufthansa, and with the secret connivance of Stalin, von Seeckt set up a training base at Lipetzk in the Soviet Union. Progress was excellent, but the new *Luftwaffe* did not get the official backing it needed until Adolf Hitler came to power in 1933. Former First World War fighter pilot Hermann Göring, last leader of von Richthofen's squadron, was appointed Air Minister, with Lufthansa chairman Erhard Milch as his deputy. By the time the *Luftwaffe* was officially unveiled to the astonished world in March 1935 its strength already stood at 20,000 officers and men, and 1888 aircraft produced by around forty different companies. The impact was exactly as Hitler intended — his potential enemies, and the world at large, were left in little doubt that Germany was rapidly developing the world's best equipped air arm. Barely a year later the Germans were completing service testing on an unprecedented eleven types of new aircraft, including the Messerschmitt 109 and 110, Junkers 87 and 88, Dornier 17, and Heinkel 111.

The Spanish Civil War

Allying with General Francisco Franco's Nationalist forces against the Republicans in order to aid the spread of fascism provided Hitler with the perfect opportunity to test his new weapons. In August 1936 six He 51 fighters and twenty Ju 52/3m transports, with eighty-five volunteer air and ground crews, were sent to Spain as the Legion Kondor. The following March the Heinkel biplanes proved themselves highly successful in attacking fortified positions with bombs, laying the foundation for the close air support doctrine that would dominate the *Luftwaffe*'s coming successes and failures. In the summer of 1937 the newest Bf 109B fighters, along with He 111 and Do 17 bombers, were also sent south. Shortly thereafter new Ju 87 and Henschel 123 dive-bombers entered combat in Spain, further underlining the *Luftwaffe*'s emphasis on ground-support. Plans for long-range heavy bombers were either dropped or given a very low priority.

Combat in Spain honed the German crews, particularly the fighter pilots, who quickly abandoned large, close formation tactics in favour of loose pairs (a *Rotte*) and flights of four (two *Rotten*, or a *Schwarm*), that were far more manoeuvrable in combat. Not only did these prove deadly, but they established a pattern for fighter tactics which lasts to this day. By the time the Germans went home in 1939, their tactics and aircraft were way ahead of those employed by any of their neighbours. In August 1939 *Luftwaffe* strength stood at 3750 front line aircraft, backed by a 25% reserve and over 3000 training aircraft (including 500 front line types for conversion training).

Poland

On 1 September 1939, Hitler ordered his armies across the Polish frontier without declaring war, thinking that none of the Western powers would want to go to war over Poland. He was wrong. On the 3rd the United Kingdom and France, after issuing an ultimatum demanding the withdrawal of German troops, declared war. As the *Wehrmacht*'s eleven Panzer and forty infantry divisions rolled across Poland, Germany's faith in the *Luftwaffe*, and dive-bombing in particular, was more than borne out by the Ju 87B Stuka's ability to destroy assigned targets. Massive formations of medium bombers with excellent fighter escort only added to the air arm's reputation for success.

The near effortless victory, due in large measure to the inadequacy of the Polish Air Force and the pinpoint use of German air power, resulted in the coining of a new term — *Blitzkrieg* or 'lightning war'. It had taken just eight days for the Panzers to reach Warsaw, where they arrived on 9 September, and on the 17th the Russians, who had signed a non-aggression pact with Germany, invaded Poland from the east. The campaign ended with the surrender of Warsaw on the 27th. The *Luftwaffe*'s success here earmarked it to become a major element in German strategy as Hitler turned west.

The Low Countries and France

After a winter of little activity, German troops, with massive air support, invaded Norway and Denmark simultaneously on 9 April 1940, encountering very little opposition. A British landing at Narvik on the 15th ended in failure, British, French and Norwegian troops being evacuated on 10 June. Without even waiting for the outcome of the fighting in Norway, Hitler had meanwhile set in motion his offensive in the West which, if things went right, would culminate in the invasion of England.

At dawn on 10 May 1940, the *Luftwaffe* struck airfields and rail and communication centres, and launched a series of airborne and glider assaults in Holland, Belgium and France. Within two days Panzers were pushing through the Ardennes, reaching the Channel coast by the 20th and thereby splitting the Allied armies in two. The *Wehrmacht* moved without any fear of aerial attack, as the *Luftwaffe* had swept all opposition from the skies with its excellent Me 109E fighter, which made short work of the Dutch, Belgian and French air forces, as well as those Royal Air Force squadrons based in France. Eventually, in a ten day period beginning on 26 May, the British Expeditionary Force and elements of the French army were evacuated by sea from the beaches of Dunkirk and De Panne under severe *Luftwaffe* bombardment.

It was over these beaches that Messerschmitt pilots encountered the Spitfire Mk I for the first time. It proved a rude shock. Here were pilots who not only knew how to fight but who flew aircraft which were in some ways superior to the 109. In combination with the equally versatile Hurricane, which hunted down bombers while the Spitfire engaged the Messerschmitts, this resulted in the *Luftwaffe*'s first significant losses of the war. Not only did this contribute significantly to the successful evacuation of Dunkirk, but it proved to be a precursor of things to come.

By 25 June 1940, the fighting in France was over. Göring assured Hitler that, after a rest and refit, his *Luftwaffe* would eliminate the Royal Air Force as an effective force while still bombing ports and shipping, thus paving the way for the invasion of England. Through June and July the Germans massed their aerial strike force on French and Belgian airfields, RAF Fighter Command using the time to rebuild its squadrons and reserves, the loss of over 100 fighters and eighty pilots over Dunkirk having reduced it to its lowest levels. Hitler's intelligence planners estimated it would take four days to neutralise British defences, and another four weeks to eliminate the RAF, with Operation *Seelöwe* (Sealion) — the invasion — set for the first two weeks in September.

The Battle of Britain and the Blitz

As the *Luftwaffe* was gathering strength it began to test RAF Fighter Command by commencing a series of modest daylight bombing attacks, beginning on 10 July 1940. The response was instant, several British squadrons engaging the Germans in a massive air battle on the very first day, with dogfights stretching across Dover. For the rest of the month the bombers continued to hit coastal targets, while the German fighters attracted their British counterparts to engage them — a tactic that could only work for so long: clearly the German bombers would have to become the main target if Britain was to survive. The RAF fighter pilots began to ditch their unwieldy 'vic' sections, based on tight formations, and to adopt the German loose pairs in flights of four. The much-vaunted Messerschmitt 110 twin-engine fighter, not as fast or as manoeuvrable as the Spitfire or Hurricane, quickly became so much meat on the table.

Göring saw he was not going to get the desired results if the British fighters would not engage his 109s. From 8 August he therefore ordered the bombers to hit targets deep in England, using his *Kampfgeschwader* (Bomber Wing) crews as bait. Over the next ten days the Ju 87 Stuka units were mauled, and after losing sixteen aircraft in a single day (18 August) they were withdrawn from the battle. *Adler Tag* (Eagle Day), the official German commencement of the Battle of Britain, was launched on the afternoon of 13 August, but it was not until the 15th that the major effort got under way, with 1786 sorties. During the next week the *Luftwaffe* pounded as many RAF airfields across southern England as it could reach, producing some of the most spectacular engagements of the battle, but also creating a grinding war of attrition. Single day losses for both sides reached their peak on 18 August. As Air Marshal Hugh Dowding, the head of RAF Fighter Command, observed during the battle, his young men would have to shoot down more of their young men in order to win.

The RAF proved far more difficult to destroy than Göring had imagined. On the 20th he issued a directive calling for more drastic action, moving as many 109s as possible forward to Pas de Calais in order to increase their short range. However, to reduce his increasing bomber losses he ordered his fighter pilots to fly very close escort. The result proved disastrous, since their tactical advantage as loose, free-hunting fighters, well developed since Spain, was neutralised, in spite of fighter sweeps designed to engage the Hurricanes and Spitfires. Even so, had Göring stayed with his plan to hit RAF bases in the south of England he may yet have succeeded, since Fighter Command, a rapidly dwindling band of worn-out pilots, was perilously close to being decimated. Aircraft could be replaced — just barely — but not experienced fighter pilots. Then Hitler unwittingly relieved the pressure.

On 2 September 1940, following an RAF raid on Berlin on 25 August, Hitler ordered the *Luftwaffe* to begin bombing British cities, and in particular London, in revenge, thinking that he could break the morale of the civilian populace. The only real results were an increase in *Luftwaffe* losses, and immediate relief for Fighter Command, which began to regain its strength following the first German raid on London on 7 September. By the 15th it was clear air superiority was not going to be achieved, and Hitler ordered *Seelöwe* postponed two days later. The invasion fleet was dispersed and sent back to Germany a month later. Göring kept his units active, but the realistic probability of a *Luftwaffe* victory over Britain was gone. To increase the bombing effort he took one *Staffel* (squadron) of 109s from each fighter *Gruppe*, along with 110s and Ju 88s, and made them fighter-bombers, while at the same time diverting most of the bombers to night attacks. This lowered losses but made accurate targeting a near impossibility. By the end of October most bombing was conducted at night and the Blitz against London and other industrial cities had started in earnest by November.

This night campaign, aimed straight at the heart of British morale, lasted until May 1941, and even though the Germans developed quite an impressive array of electronic bombing aids, substantially increasing their accuracy,

the main result was a strengthening of British resolve to not only last through the Blitz but to strike back. With no tangible results in the West, Hitler turned his attention East, withdrawing *Luftwaffe* units to Germany and eastern Poland in readiness for an invasion of the Soviet Union. A reduced force of bomber, fighter and anti-shipping units was left in the occupied countries of Western Europe, but even these were continually reduced for operations in Russia and the Mediterranean. Hitler was confident he would defeat Russia by the end of the year, and would then return and deal with Britain.

The continental air war

As RAF Bomber Command stepped up its night attacks against German cities, the *Luftwaffe* responded by creating an increasingly impressive night fighter arm, which graduated from single engine Messerschmitt 109s to radar-equipped 110s, Ju 88s and Do 215s with formidable fire-power. In many ways the significant air battles of the western air war were fought at night well into 1943, with the electronics wizards of both sides rapidly developing ingeniously sophisticated equipment virtually from scratch. Bomber Command's first 'thousand bomber raid' on Cologne on the night of 30—31 May 1942 was also a harbinger of things to come, though after two more such massive raids it proved impossible to put this many bombers up again until 1944.

Despite the assignment of the outstanding Focke-Wulf Fw 190 single engine fighter to Channel Coast day fighter units in the late-summer of 1941, numerous teething problems prevented its full deployment until the following year. Although German *Jagdgeschwader* (Fighter Wing) pilots continued to duel with RAF Fighter Command as both sides made thrusts and parries across the Channel, the air war in the West gradually dwindled as the *Luftwaffe* suffered from increasing demands for its services on multiple fronts. Not until the American daylight bombing campaign, which began in August 1942 and gained strength throughout 1943, would Hitler be forced to refocus the *Luftwaffe*'s attentions on the West.

Above: When the war began in September 1939 the Messerschmitt 109 was the finest fighter in the world. After a long development period, which involved honing combat capability during the Spanish Civil War, the 109 was already famous long before the invasion of Poland. This Me 109E was attached to *Jagdfliegerschule* (Fighter Pilot School) 1 at Werneuchen during the winter of 1939—40, when the 'Emil' was being introduced into service. (*Alex Stöcker* via *Herrmann & Kraemer*)

Below: In spite of its slow speed and fixed undercarriage, the Junkers 52/3m remained the *Luftwaffe*'s primary transport right up to the end of the Second World War. It became an integral part of Germany's pioneering airborne operations, dropping troops into battle by parachute from the very first days of the Polish campaign.

Left: High summer 1940 found the war being fought in the skies over Britain. A *Jagdgeschwader* 2 Messerschmitt 109E-3 rests at its field in France awaiting the next mission across the Channel, with the *Jagdverbande* (Fighter Arm) flag flying in the foreground. *Luftwaffe* fighter pilots found themselves at the end of their fuel limits to fight effectively over England. (*Herrmann & Kraemer*)

Below left: A Messerschmitt 110C, well hidden by natural camouflage, is readied for a sortie early in the war. When the Bf 110 was initially delivered to line units it was greatly hoped that it would prove an effective *Zerstörer* or heavy fighter, able to escort bomber formations. The opposite proved to be true over England, where its crews found themselves easy targets for Spitfire and Hurricane pilots.

Below: As war broke out in Europe the Luftwaffe represented one of the finest working military machines in existence, with well trained personnel and excellent equipment. Several ground crew refuel this Hienkel 111 with no effort thanks to good support vehicles and properly defined roles. This situation would carry the Luftwaffe through the early years until training and manpower were cut to the bone.

Opposite page, top: When the Henschel 126 appeared in mid-1938 it was the *Luftwaffe*'s first modern all-metal tactical reconnaissance aircraft. During the Polish campaign Hs 126 *Aufklärungsstaffeln* (reconnaissance squadrons) assigned to each army corps became integral to command planning, able to give field generals a rapid and accurate view of the battles they were fighting. By 1942 the 126 had been replaced, primarily by the Fw 189.

Left: Pilots confer in front of their Messerschmitt 109s before a mission. One of the aircraft's major advantages in combat against Spitfires and Hurricanes during 1940 was the ability to abruptly push over into a dive. The Daimler Benz engine's fuel injection system was not subject to gravity so operated well at negative Gs, while British carburettors would starve an engine of fuel in the same manoeuvre.

Above: One of Germany's pre-war airliners developed into a bomber, the Fw 200 had such impressive range that zealous planners made the mistake of demanding too much of it. The landing gear and fuselage were too weak to carry full military loads from the outset, leading to collapsed undercarriages and broken backs throughout its history.

An armourer fits the forward-firing 7.92 mm machine-gun to the nose of his Heinkel 111H. The *Luftwaffe*'s primary bomber during the early war years, the He 111 had six defensive guns in various positions, but they were woefully inadequate. With a bomb load of 2000 kg (4410 lbs) or two torpedoes, the aircraft could be quite lethal, but without fighter escort it was impossible to avoid heavy losses.

Above: A new Messerschmitt 109F shares the line with one of its older 'Emil' brothers in the late winter slush of 1941. Several units had started to get the 109F by the middle of the year, and found it to have better high-altitude performance than the Spitfire, but at the cost of reduced armament. Many *Luftwaffe* fighter pilots thought it was a step backwards, but the F nevertheless ended up doing quite well in all theatres.

Below: III/JG 2 Messerschmitt 109Es wait in line in France. The red 'R' in a white shield, the *Geschwader*'s emblem, stood for Richthofen, the famous First World War ace, a name the pilots were proud to carry into battle.

Above: The resurgence of German nationalism in the 1920s and 1930s led to an enormous expansion of the dormant aircraft industry. Former First World War ace Gerhard Fieseler (twenty-two kills) became an aerobatics champion, and then formed his own company. Here he runs up his personal aircraft, an F 2 Tiger biplane, the company's first powered aircraft designed by Ing. Schüttkowsky. Fieseler won the 1934 World Aerobatics Championship and 80,000 marks flying this aircraft. (*Peter Petrick*)

Right: The Spanish Civil War proved invaluable to *Luftwaffe* pilots in developing their combat skills. It was in Spain that many of the coming war's most famous aircraft were tested, including the Bf 109. These new 109Es, flying with *Jagdgruppe* (Fighter Group) 88 of the Legion Kondor in March 1939, were far ahead of anything else fielded during the conflict.

Above: The early two-bladed Bf 109s, like this C photographed before the outbreak of war, were difficult to handle, both in the air and on the ground. Many pilots from the biplane era, including General Ernst Udet, thought an enclosed cockpit would hinder the pilot's abilities in a dogfight. The leap in technology was difficult to fathom on many levels.

Below: 'Red 6', a Bf 109C-2 with 2/JG 2 (2 *Staffel* of *Jagdgeschwader* 2), gets some quick line maintenance and fuel at Friedrichshafen in 1939. Ease of field maintenance was among the outstanding features of the 109. The fuel hoses could lock straight into the fuel tank necks, well displayed here, a feature that would not become standard until the jet age. The undercarriage was mounted to a solid box built into the fuselage, which meant that the wings could be removed without jacking the aircraft off the ground.

Above: The first slender-fuselage Dornier 17s deserved their nickname of the 'Flying Pencil'. These Do 17Ps from 2 *Staffel* of *Fernaufklärungsgruppe* (Long-range Reconnaissance Group) 11 warm up at Grossenhain in August 1939, just before the beginning of the war. Though this version of the aircraft was built specifically for long-range reconnaissance it would slowly evolve through several different versions with enlarged fuselages until it could perform a number of missions in addition to bombing, including night fighting. (*Heinz Nowarra* via *Peter Petrick*)

Below: 'Yellow 14', an Me 109E of 6/(J)186T (about to be redesignated JG 77) at Nordholz, December 1939, carried quite a striking example of personal artwork. Though the Germans were not recognised for individual art on their aircraft, the practice was quite widespread. (*Peter Petrick*)

Above: One of the three Blohm und Voss Ha 140 torpedo-bomber seaplane prototypes during a test flight in the late-1930s. The *Reichsluftfahrtministerium* (or RLM, the German Aviation Ministry) initiated many different seaplane projects before the Second World War and the *Luftwaffe* maintained quite an ambitious seaplane capability, from massive flying boats to small scout float planes. Losing out in competition to the He 115, the Ha 140 programme was cancelled in September 1939. (*George Petersen*)

Below: Another stillborn Blohm und Voss project, the Ha 139 long-range seaplane appeared as three prototypes, beginning in late-1936. The three aircraft were used extensively, making several transatlantic flights powered by four Junkers Jumo 205 diesel engines, before being modified for *Luftwaffe* use. The Ha 139V3 became the Ha 139B, pictured here, and served as a logistical support aircraft and a minesweeper. Lack of spares grounded it after 1942. (*George Petersen*)

Above: At the time of the invasion of Poland on 1 September 1939 the *Luftwaffe* had the only effective transport and airborne force in the world. The trusty Ju 52 proved pivotal to the *Blitzkrieg*, carrying both supplies and *Falschirmjäger* (airborne troops) into battle. (*George Petersen*)

Right: *Falschirmjäger* jump from a Ju 52 of KGrzbV 9 in an attack on Lwow on 24 September 1939, only three days before the Polish campaign ended with the fall of Warsaw. (KGrzbV stands for *Kampfgruppe zur besonderen Verwendung,* or Special Duties Battle Group.) With total air superiority, the slow transports could operate with impunity, something *Luftwaffe* generals got used to. It would eventually cost them dearly. (*George Petersen*)

Opposite page, top: During the Polish campaign personal aircraft art proliferated, often with messages telling the enemy what they could expect. The crew of this Ju 52 in Poland left no doubts as to their sentiments: '1.9.39 — Whether men, fuel, bombs or bread, we bring death to Poland'. The open turret on top of the cockpit was one of many self-defence modifications added to *Alte Tante Ju* ('Old Aunt Ju', the affection-ate nickname given to the Ju 52). (*Peter Petrick*)

Above: Autumn 1939 — A ground crewman paints a *Kleine Fische* emblem on the nose of his Me 109E, a sentiment the pilot surely agreed with since the meaning translates roughly as 'no problem', or in RAF parlance 'a piece of cake'. *Luftwaffe* fighter pilots certainly had no problem dealing with enemy aircraft during the first six months of the war, shooting entire air forces out of the sky from Poland through the Low Countries to France. That would change drastically as 1940 unfolded, beginning over the beaches of Dunkirk. (*Peter Petrick*)

Left: Werner Mölders, then *Staffelkapitän* (squadron commander) of 8/JG 51, jumps into his Me 109E during an *Alarmstart* (scramble). The engine is running, having been started by the ground crew — as soon as they strap him in and pull the metal chocks, all the pilot has to do is shove the throttle forward and be off. *Luftwaffe* air and ground crews operated like well-oiled machinery, even in the worst of times later in the war.

Above: These *Schwartze* of 3/*Stukageschwader* (Stuka Wing) 1 watch their Ju 87B-2s taxi in from a mission against a Polish target in September 1939. The campaign established the reputation of the Junkers dive-bomber for accuracy and for creating terror among those being attacked on the ground. In an environment of total aerial supremacy, the Stuka (an abbreviation of *Sturzkampfflugzeug*, or dive-bomber) was a fantastic tactical weapon. The result of Ernst Udet's obsession with dive-bombing, it flew for the first time in 1935.

Below: The shark mouth on this Ju 87B-2 of II/StG 77 (II *Gruppe* of *Stukageschwader* 77) was a propaganda effort rather than a unit emblem. The idea was to capitalise on the aircraft's fearsome reputation earned during the Polish campaign, which was enhanced by the air-driven siren mounted to the exterior of one undercarriage leg. Between bombing and strafing, the *Stukageschwaderen* were the stars of the first several months of the war. (*Peter Petrick*)

Above: A flight of three *Stabs Staffel* (staff squadron) Ju 87B-1s of StG 2 head for a target in the Polish haze, September 1939. Just about all the protection a Stuka needed during these early campaigns was the rear-gunner, since most enemy fighters had about the same performance.

Below: With an empty bomb carriage, a 1/StG 1 Ju 87B-1 returns from a mission over Poland in September 1939. Handling was first-class, according to most pilots, with excellent controls and an automatic pull-out system which did quite well if a pilot blacked out (a rare occurrence).

Right: Bombed-up with a central 500 kg bomb and 50 kg bombs under the wings, two Stukas of 10/LG 1 (10 *Staffel* of *Lehrgeschwader* or Training Wing 1) climb out from Mannheim on the way to their targets in Alsace, 21 June 1940. (*NASM*)

Below: Junkers 52s from 6/KGzbV 2 (6 *Staffel* of *Kampfgeschwader zur besonderen Verwendung* 2) fly across Poland unmolested during the *Blitzkrieg* of September 1939, when it came into its own with some 550 in service. From that point on *Tante Ju* was everywhere and was particularly crucial to keeping German armies in Russia and North Africa supplied. Unfortunately, she was also a sitting duck at her 200 kph (124 mph) cruising speed and great numbers were downed by Allied fighters, often carrying hundreds of troops to their death.

Opposite page, bottom: The rough fields of Poland proved no problem for Me 109s, which were designed to fly from grass. This I/LG 2 Me 109E warms up while awaiting his leader in September 1939. The 109s made mincemeat of everything the enemy flew until meeting British fighters over the beaches of Dunkirk. (*Richard Lutz* via *Barry Rosch*)

Above: Secretly test-flown as a bomber in February 1935, the He 111 prototype was labelled an airliner to hide its purpose. In February 1937 the He 111B entered combat with the Legion Kondor in Spain and was quite effective, a success that would later cost the *Luftwaffe* dearly. The last of the early model Heinkel 111s, with a stepped-up cockpit, were being phased out of front line service when this one from *Stab* I/KG (*Kampfgeschwader*) 1 was seen in Poland in September 1939.

Below: A fast aircraft for its day, the He 111 was considered to have adequate defensive armament, which was true for the early months of the war. Pilots enjoyed flying it very much and it could take a fair amount of battle damage and still stay in the air. This 10/KG 1 He 111H-1 has just released its load over Poland. The dorsal gunner had quite a field of view, but the aircraft's 7.92 mm machine-guns were not all that effective at long range.

Opposite page, top: The crew of a *Stab*/KG 1 He 111H-1 relax before a mission over Poland. Because of their pre-war experience in Spain, German combat personnel were amongst the most experienced in the world. The successful invasion of Poland, due in no small measure to the *Luftwaffe*, engendered a sense of invincibility, which was an unhealthy disposition to take into battle for any length of time.

Opposite page, bottom: When Germany invaded Norway and Denmark on 9 April 1940 there was only token resistance, and both nations quickly succumbed despite British and French intervention. These I/StG 1 crews at Sola Airfield, Stavanger, Norway, seem to reflect the pace of the campaign. The Ju 87B-2, marked with 3 *Staffel*'s diving raven, is bombed-up and ready. The *Staffel* banner has been erected as well. (*Knut Maesel* via *Barry Rosch*)

Above: Germany's most notorious propaganda *Geschwader* flew 'Heinkel 113s', here lined up and ready for battle in the spring of 1940 according to a Berlin press release. In reality, the aircraft were nine of the twelve early production He 100D-1s painted alike in several different fictitious unit markings and then re-photographed. The intention was to convince the world that the aircraft was entering large scale service, and throughout the war Allied pilots reported encountering it, though it never entered line service other than as part of the factory defence force at Marienehe.

Below: During May 1940 10(N)/JG 2 deployed older Bf 109C-2s to Värnes airfield, Norway, during the very early stages of *Luftwaffe* attempts to form a night fighter deterrent against RAF Bomber Command. The *Staffel* would later become a part of NJG 1, a fully-fledged night fighting unit. (*Ken Merrick* via *Barry Rosch*)

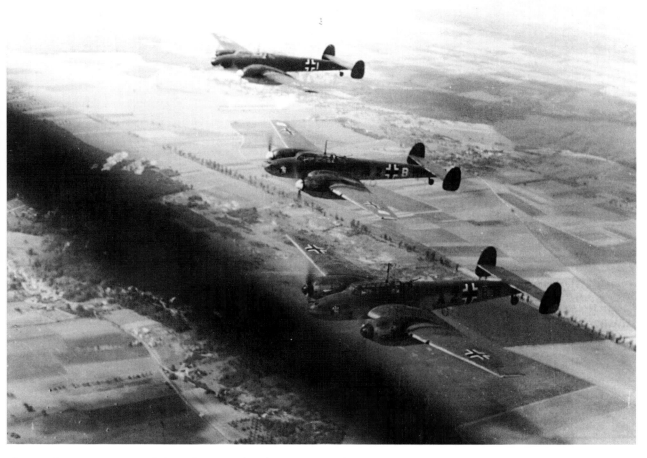

Above: When Me 110s moved through France their heavy firepower was quite effective against anything in front of them. These I/ZG 52 Me 110Cs flying across the French countryside have been repainted for the coming campaign against Britain. The older, dark green splinter camouflage stood out like a black blob even at medium altitudes, so the Germans issued a new series of specifications to blend aircraft into the hazy air-to-air combat background.

Below: Two Me 110Cs warm up at their 1/ZG 52 airfield in Charleville, France, 1940. Through the *Blitzkrieg* in the West the Messerschmitt 110 was quite a successful fighter and crew morale was very high. Few of the woefully inadequate enemy fighters it faced could compete with it, in large measure due to the German crews' combat experience.

Above: A 2/ZG 52 Messerschmitt 110C-4 taking off from Charleville, France, in 1940. The flaps are lowered about ten degrees for increased lift and the elevators are still slightly nose-down to keep the main undercarriage stuck to the grass. This technique kept the aircraft very controllable until the pilot decided to ease back on the stick and let it become airborne. The rudders are deflected to the right, to counter the propeller effect popularly known as torque.

Below: Summer 1940: During the early stages of the Battle of Britain, 1/KG 3 Dornier 17Z-1 crews wait for the last of their aircraft to be fuelled for a sortie against England from their airfield at Le Culot. The field facilities are excellent, with underground pits and ground power units. The bomber's enlarged crew compartment was designed to make the aircraft more effective, but the modification increased drag and rendered it underpowered. As a result the bomb load had to be reduced to a paltry 500 kg.

Above: The Ju 88 flew for the first time in December 1936 and was immediately regarded as the ideal *Schnellbomber* (high-speed bomber) around which to build the growing *Luftwaffe*. Entering service just days after the start of the Second World War, it quickly became an airframe modified for many different missions — more than any other German wartime aircraft, as it turned out. Here a 3/KG 51 'Edelweiss' Ju 88A-1 is readied for combat at its excellent Melun-Villaroche airfield in France, 1940.

Right: German design philosophy located most of the multi-engine bomber crew in the nose. This was excellent for crew co-ordination but could become somewhat of a liability since concentrated fire from an attacking fighter could wipe out everyone aboard in short order.

Above: A 9/KG 53 Heinkel 111H-1, flying from Lille, France, heads for England in the summer of 1940. A temporary formation marking, three white bars, was often repeated as two bars on the rudder. Though the bomber's nose was certainly streamlined, the multiple glass panels were actually difficult to see through and often reflected sunlight back into the cockpit.

Opposite page, top: The idyllic *Luftwaffe* bases in France were excellent for launching the assault on Britain, not only in maintenance facilities but in crew quarters. A 1/KG 54 Ju 88A-1 warms up at Evreaux before heading for England.

During the initial stages of the Battle of Britain, German morale and confidence were high.

Below: A stricken Do 17Z. With its right engine on fire, it begins to roll over and then goes down as the pilot fights for control. Most twin engine aircraft of the period were difficult to handle on one engine — if the aircraft slowed down too much, the good engine would roll it over unless the pilot either reduced power or lowered the nose to gain speed. Managing either when badly hit was often impossible. (*George Petersen*)

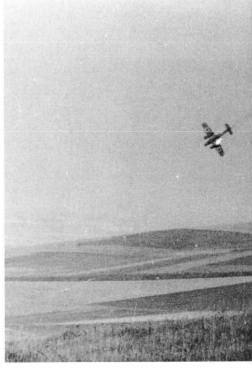

Above: In loose formation, Do 17Zs from 3/KG 76 head across France unmolested. Once over the Channel the formation leader will call for his pilots to close up for mutual cover from the defensive 7.92mm machine-guns in each aircraft. As things turned out, the relative ease of previous campaigns did not prepare the Germans for the tenacity and accuracy of defending British fighter pilots, who would press on through any amount of fire to get at the bombers.

Below: A 1/KG 3 Do 17Z climbs out for a raid on England. In spite of its underpowered nature and relatively small bomb load, the Dornier was a major cog in German pre-invasion 'softening up' operations. As Göring was to find out, every aircraft at his disposal was needed to hit the RAF airfields. The Dorniers were occasionally sent in at low level, though the two *Staffeln* which specialised in such attacks also flew standard bombing missions. (*George Petersen*)

Above: The Junkers 88 was considered the most effective of the *Luftwaffe*'s medium bombers, not just during the Battle of Britain, but throughout the war. The crew of this KG 51 aircraft has quite an effective load lined up for their aircraft, which could carry 500 kg bombs internally and 1000 kg bombs on external racks. The real problem faced by the German crews, as with those of other nations, was placing the bombs accurately on significant targets. (*George Petersen*)

Below: As this Do 17Z and Me 109E have demonstrated on a field in France, operational accidents took a heavy toll on men and machines. In the far background is one of 50 *Regia Aeronautica* Fiat CR.42 biplane fighters sent to aid the *Luftwaffe* from October 1940 to January 1941. It was hopelessly outclassed. (*George Petersen*)

Above: *Zerstörergeschwader* 76's II *Gruppe* was famous for painting a number of different versions of shark's teeth on its Me 110s and was eventually nicknamed the *Haifisch* (Shark) *Gruppe*. Pilots on the Allied side often copied this fashion, the most famous examples being the Tomahawks flown in the Western Desert by the RAF's 112 Squadron, and in China by the American Volunteer Group, Claire Chennault's Flying Tigers. Like the 110, the nose shape of the Curtiss Tomahawk proved ideally suited to this colourful style of decoration. (*Peter Petrick*)

Below: Junkers 88s of KG 51 climb out over France. Pilots universally loved flying all models of this very effective medium bomber. Not only was it fast, but it handled quite well in all conditions, one of the reasons it could be adapted to so many roles. (*George Petersen*)

Above: The clean lines of this Ju 88A-5 attached to KG 77 reveal the reason for the aircraft's success. When bombs were hung on underwing shackles to increase its effective punch, top speed went down — but not by much. The 88 still had the performance needed to be effective in combat, particularly once the bombs were gone.

Below: The pastoral tranquillity at Lille, France, is broken by running Junkers Jumo 1300 hp V-12s as 1/KG 53 taxies out for targets in England. The flat French countryside was ideal for combat operations, with not just operational military airfields but multiple emergency landing fields dotted about everywhere.

Left: One of the many personal pilot emblems in JG 26 adorns the side of a *Geschwader* Me 109E. Much of the art was quite detailed, reflecting the pilot's individual tastes. Clearly this one thought himself a tiger in the air, as so many of the 109 pilots were. The *Luftwaffe* fighter corps quickly became *Experten*, or experts, at their trade. (*Peter Petrick*)

Below: A III/JG 26 'Schlageter' pilot jumps from his Me 109E at Caffiers, France, after a sortie. The gravel taxiways were frequently rough on propellers, lowered flaps, and radiators, but that was often the only alternative to getting bogged down in mud.

Above: Major Adolf Galland, commander of III *Gruppe*, JG 26, prepares for a mission from Caffiers during the pivotal late-summer of 1940. A legendary pilot, Galland was one of the leading *Experten* during the Battle of Britain, later going on to become General of Fighters in the *Luftwaffe*, a position he considered more difficult than combat flying.

Below: Now *Kommodore* of JG 26, Adolf Galland makes his way across the gravel taxi strip at Wissant, France, in September 1940. Galland found the Me 109E-4 an excellent fighter in most respects except range. He was famous for arguing with Göring about how ill-equipped his fighter pilots were to fight a long-range war over England, particularly when they wasted fuel trying to stay with the bombers. External drop tanks could have tilted the battle in Germany's favour.

Above: Several Me 109E-4s from 6/JG 53 line the field at Brest, summer 1940. Typical of most *Luftwaffe Geschwader,* the unit's *Gruppen* were spread across several airfields — I at Rennes, II at Dinan, and III at Brest — while the commander, Major Hans-Jurgen von Cramon-Taubel, ran the *Geschwader* from Cherbourg. Each *Gruppe* acted as a self-contained entity, able to move and act without a great deal of higher level interference.

Below: I and II/JG 77 Me 109E-3s are readied for combat at their airfield in France. Field maintenance on most Messerschmitts was predictable and relatively uncomplicated. The aircraft were built for forward base operations and mechanics found them simple to work with once the systems were mastered. (*Simon Perry* via *Barry Rosch*)

Above: With radiator exit air-shutters full open for maximum cooling, a formation of 7/KG 1 Heinkel 111H-2s climbs out from its base at Montdidier, France, summer 1940. The underwing codes, which used to be BD, have been painted out, but the new codes, IR, have only been placed on the fuselage. As *Luftwaffe* losses mounted, aircraft were shuffled between units to put up as many full strength formations as possible.

Below: When daytime bomber losses became prohibitive in the later stages of the Battle of Britain, Göring switched to night attacks. Just how rapidly this was done is reflected in the painting-out by hand of all bright markings on this 4/KG 54 Ju 88A-1 at St Andre, France. There was no time to worry about neatness, which would only come when the factories could paint new aircraft during assembly.

Right: The aircraft of I/JG 77's adjutant is in the process of being refitted, high summer 1940. The *Hellblau* (light blue) camouflage was ordered to be extended from the undersurfaces to the entire side of all fighters just as the Battle of Britain was developing. This made aircraft blend far better into their higher altitude air-to-air environment, a concept which revealed the Germans' grasp of how colour worked in various lighting conditions. These particular aircraft have the 'over-water' paint scheme introduced in about July 1940 for units involved in longer Channel crossings (such as from Cherbourg to Portsmouth).

Above: The *Schwartze* have only had time to paint out some of the markings on these II/KG 55 He 111P-2s being switched over to night bombing. Losses certainly went down when daytime raids were halted, but so did accuracy. The Germans pioneered the use of electronic aids for night operations during the Blitz, but no sooner had a system been perfected than the British came up with a countermeasure — and vice versa.

Below: Bombs are carried to a Do 17Z by hand during the late afternoon of 12 December 1940, as the night Blitz against England reaches its height. The RAF, while launching its own night bombing effort, also began to counter the *Luftwaffe* with an ever-increasing night fighter force. Both sides were soon quite adept at combat in the dark. (*George Petersen*)

Above: 'Jaguar!' was the pilot's name for this Messerschmitt 110 of *Erprobungsgruppe* 210 at Köln-Ostheim, Germany, September 7, 1940. This evaluation unit proved weapons additions and modifications to the Me 110 while getting ready for the first Me 210s. In spite of the 110 factory line being shut down, the desperate need for night fighters gave the aircraft a new lease of life and it was ordered back into production for use in that role. (*Peter Petrick*)

Right: The well-known emblem of I/ZG 26 — a snorting, winged German alligator in hot pursuit of a helpless British fish — did not reflect the reality of the Me 110's failure over England. Initially assigned the job of sweeping away the opposition ahead of the bomber stream, *Zerstörer* (destroyer, or heavy fighter) crews found themselves at the mercy of English single engine fighters.

Above: The Blitz, autumn 1940: A He 111P-6 of III/KG 55 has been daubed with quite a bit of impromptu night camouflage, with the black undersurfaces extended up the sides on the rear fuselage.

Below: The witch motif on this Heinkel 111 of 5/AufklGr (F) (*Aufklärungsgruppe (fern)*, or Long-range Reconnaissance Group) 122 was strictly a whim of the crew, which probably felt as if it was riding a broomstick in consequence of the long-range reconnaissance missions normally assigned to the unit.

Right and below: Several crews in KG 55 had unique personal art painted on their Heinkels, from an ineffective defensive umbrella which could not prevent 500 kg bombs from falling on London, to *Unteroffizier* Ritter ('Knight') holding a Crusader's banner and a bomb. (*Peter Petrick*)

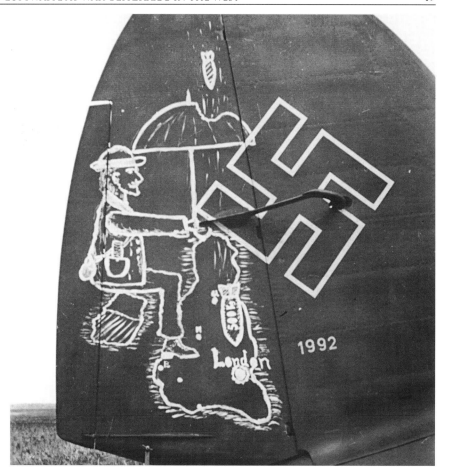

Above: The crew's artwork on this 1/KG 55 He 111 represented 'the bull of Scapa Flow', a reference to the British naval base in the Orkney Islands. The ships coming and going from here were prime targets for *Luftwaffe* aircraft and *Kriegsmarine* U-boats. (*Kroll* via *Peter Petrick*)

Below: The sentiments of this *Luftlandgeschwader* (Air Landing Wing) 2 crew seem to be clear enough as they 'moon' the enemy. The Germans seem to have had a great deal of freedom in painting personal art and names on their aircraft. Only the Americans would top them a few years later. (*Heinz Nowarra* via *Peter Petrick*)

Above: This Heinkel 111 came to grief near Prague on 16 July 1941. The factory-style codes indicate that the aircraft had not yet been assigned to a combat unit or had only just been delivered. Czechoslovakia, annexed by Hitler before the war, was a perfect staging point for the *Blitzkrieg* — certainly something that he calculated in his plans. (*George Petersen*)

Below: When the first Me 109Fs were delivered to operational units in January 1941 the differences from the well-liked E were more than evident. The aircraft had been cleaned up aerodynamically and top speed went from 355 mph to 390 mph. However, cannon armament was reduced from three 20 mm in the E-3 to a single 15 mm cannon in the F-3, while both models had two 7.92 mm machine-guns in the cowling. Many pilots complained, but the F was a fine fighter, better than the Spitfire V it faced. (*George Petersen*)

With the switch to night bombing in October 1940, Göring explored every available means of carrying extra bombs to England. Looking once again to his fighter pilots, he ordered one *Staffel* from each *Gruppe* to be turned into a fighter-bomber unit, equipped with Me 109s modified to carry bombs. These fast, low level intruder missions did little damage, but they did hamper the fighter *Geschwaderen* from doing their primary job and, in the end, actually hurt the *Luftwaffe* war effort.

Above: As early as 1937 Willy Messerschmitt was working on a successor to the Bf 110, but the Me 210 V1 did not fly until 1 September 1939. From the start the aircraft was a disappointment and, in a move typical of *Luftwaffe* mismanagement, 1000 were ordered into production before the prototype had flown. By the end of 1940 Me 210As were reaching their destined units, and almost immediately accident rates started increasing. Production was finally halted in April 1942 after 200 had been delivered, 370 more were on the production line, and components existed for another 800. Erhard Milch demanded Messerschmitt's resignation, but the famous designer had far too much power by then.

Below: An obsolete second-line Do 17E-1 after a landing accident at Prague Ruzyn airfield in 1941. As the *Luftwaffe* continued to expand, older versions of its aircraft were withdrawn to serve as trainers or utility aircraft. This version of Dornier's famous bomber was first assigned to front line units in early-1937 so it was quite long in the tooth by 1941. (*George Petersen*)

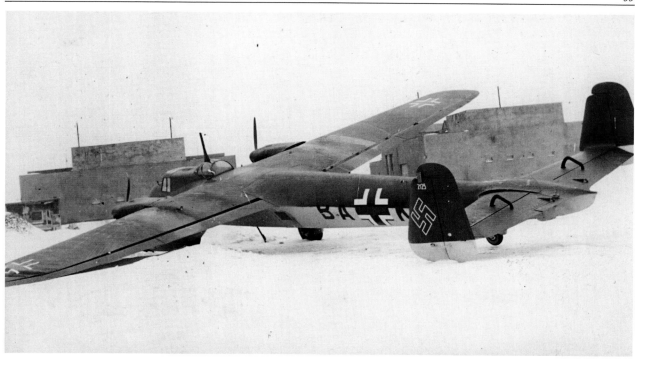

Opposite page, top: One of the constant problems to dog combat pilots during the Second World War was the operation of tailwheel configured aircraft, which meant almost all aircraft in service. Not only were they unstable on landing and take off, but too much brake or a small ditch would put them on their noses, with the result exhibited by this Ju 87B at Prague Ruzyn on 13 March 1941. This particular accident most likely occurred while taxiing at low power since only a single propeller blade has buried itself in the ground and the other two are straight. (*George Petersen*)

Opposite page, bottom: When a tailwheel was fitted nose-over accidents took place with no regard for the size of the aircraft. The snow was just too much for this Heinkel 111 and its crew. (*George Petersen*)

Above and below: More snow accidents at Prague Ruzyn in February 1942 have damaged older models of the Do 17 and Ju 86. Even though the aircraft are relatively unharmed, with just a bent outer left wing tip on the 17 and some bent prop blades on both, their age may very well doom them to the scrap heap. Before too long, however, the *Luftwaffe* would be so hard pressed that anything flyable was of value. (*George Petersen*)

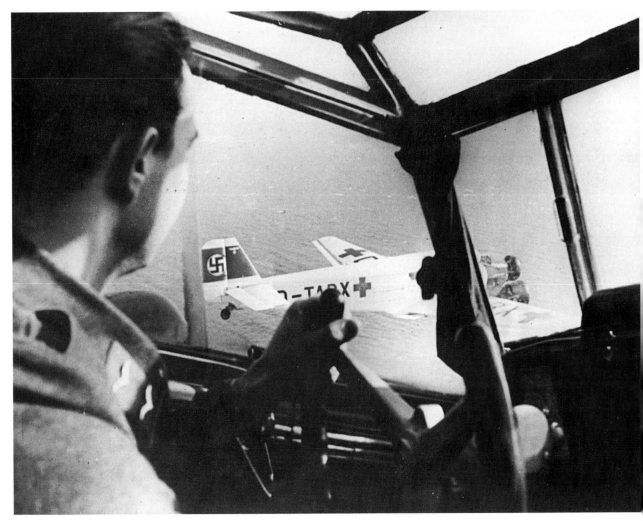

Opposite page, top: Salvaging much of the tooling and jigs from the Me 210, Messerschmitt changed the designation to 410 to avoid the political fall-out and produced quite a successful multi-role *Kampfzerstörer*. At last there was an improvement over the 110. After becoming operational in early-1943, the 410 served in fighter-bomber, bomber-destroyer, reconnaissance, maritime strike, and fast bomber roles. These 410As belong to the *Stabschwarm* of II/ZG 76. (*Peter Petrick*)

Opposite page, bottom: A pair of Ju 52s, with the clear red crosses of ambulance/rescue aircraft, fly patrol over the ocean. By the terms of the Geneva Convention aircraft and vehicles bearing such markings were theoretically supposed to be immune from attack, but quite often this ideal was not realised in practice. (*George Petersen*)

Above: A well-worn Bf 109C, now serving as a fighter lead-in transition trainer, rests at a field in Germany in late-1942 or early-1943. According to most pilots who flew 109s, the earlier models were much harder to handle on the ground. Even though later versions still had the narrow undercarriage, other design changes helped the pilot quite a bit. If someone could fly a B, C, or D in training, he was probably sufficiently qualified to fly the later versions in combat. (*George Petersen*)

Below: A Dornier Do 26V4, attached to the *Sonderstaffel* (special squadron) of *Küstenfliegergruppe* (Coastal Reconnaissance Group) 406, patrols just off the coast of Norway in 1940. The *Luftwaffe* was well-equipped for coastal reconnaissance with a fine variety of seaplanes. The movements of British convoys were constantly dogged by German reconnaissance and bomber seaplanes. (*George Petersen*)

Above: The Focke-Wulf 189's appearance was so unusual that it was nicknamed *Die Fliegende Auge* ('the flying eye'). Powered by two small Argus 465 hp engines, the 189 had one primary purpose — to support the ground troops as a tactical reconnaissance and army co-operation machine. By the end of 1941 it was replacing the Hs 126 as the primary equipment for the *Luftwaffe*'s *Aufklärungsstaffeln* (reconnaissance squadrons).

Below: Major Siegfried Schnell, *Kapitän* of 6/JG 2, flew Me 109F-4 'Yellow 9' out of Théville, France, in May 1942. By this time the *Luftwaffe* and the RAF were sparring with each other back and forth across the Channel more than anything

else. Fighter sweeps from both sides went in search of prey in a war of attrition which had no more definite goal than to wear the other side down.

Opposite page, top and bottom: Adolf Galland's personal Siebel Fh 104 liaison transport carried all the emblems under his command or of the units he visited. Here he climbs aboard, then fires up the left engine at Bergen am See in January 1942. The art represents JG 51, Erg.Schl.Gr., JG 52, JG 3, Schl.6 and II/JG 1. Galland remained one of the most popular *Luftwaffe* commanders throughout the war. (*Peter Petrick*)

Right: From the time it entered combat in June 1940 as a *Fernkampfflugzeug* or patrol bomber, the Condor was, according to Winston Churchill, the 'scourge of the Atlantic', sinking Allied shipping far out to sea beyond the reach of protective fighter cover. Despite a gradual increase in the Allies' ability to intercept and down them, Fw 200s were continually upgraded, finally carrying search radar and Hs 293 guided missiles to assist in their hunt for shipping. (*George Petersen*)

Below: Mounting losses finally forced the *Luftwaffe* to turn the Fw 200 back into its intended role as a transport. Even so, the small total production run of 276 (the last was built in February 1944) was way out of proportion to the aircraft's impressive lethality, since it seemed to roam the Atlantic at will with great success. (*George Petersen*)

Opposite page, bottom: The only combat version of the Condor built, the Fw 200C, was flown almost exclusively by one unit, KG 40, operating from airfields in France, where this 8 *Staffel* C-4 has been readied for a mission. The results achieved far outweighed the minor scale of the Condor effort, yielding one of Germany's most successful and least costly military aviation programmes, in spite of the aircraft's structural weakness.

In spite of years of development following the appearance of the first He 177 mock-up in November 1937, a rabidly determined Ernst Heinkel watched the overly complex 'Greif' (Griffin) fail as Germany's major purpose-developed long-range four engine strategic bomber. The two monstrous Daimler Benz engines were actually four 12-cylinder powerplants coupled into two 24-cylinder blocks. Many innovations far ahead of their time appeared throughout the aircraft, which entered combat evaluation with IV/KG 40 in France in the summer of 1941. (*George Petersen*)

Above: A *Kette* or flight of three fighters (4/KG 40 Do 217E-4s) races across France at low level in late-1942 or early-1943. The night bombing campaign against Britain had a fine aircraft in the redesigned Dornier 217E, which was re-engined with BMW 801s. KG 40 had a variety of aircraft at its disposal, including the unique He 177 and the Fw 200, to keep Hitler's offensive campaign running in spite of his increasing need for defensive fighters.

Below: When NJG 1 (*Nachtjagdgeschwader* or Night Fighter Wing 1) was formed, many of its Me 110s retained their day camouflage finishes, but before long solid black became the

standard colour. This 110E is not fitted with radar, but crews managed to get several kills through vectoring by ground control, which would put them within visual range of their targets. Needless to say, one needed a pretty clear moonlit or starlit night for this to work. (*Simon Perry* via *Barry Rosch*)

Opposite page: Two cement 250 kg practice bombs are hung on an Me 110 of *Erg.Schl.Gruppe* before a training sortie. The 110 was tested as a ground attack aircraft, but other types did the job far better. The only new lease of life for the type came with the growing night fighter war. (*Peter Petrick*)

Above: A *Schwartze* and one of his aircrew stand next to their 5/NJG 3 Me 110 at Esbjerg on 23 August 1941. Early night fighter crews on both sides were determined, talented men who considered innovation a norm in the dark skies over Europe.

Below: A *Rotte* of Me 110Es from 8/NJG 4 fly across France during the winter of 1942—3. The bright markings have been painted out by hand and the camouflage dappled more than usual to enhance the aircraft's' chances of survival when attacking RAF bombers. The British gunners, particularly those manning rear turrets, became quite adept at spotting, and hitting, 110s that crept up from behind in the dark. Tactics continually changed, but the first major leap forward was the installation of onboard radar.

Above: Night fighting camouflage was standardised during 1942, as these two Me 110Es from 7/NJG 4 demonstrate over France. After its poor showing during the Battle of Britain — and anywhere else that enemy fighters were dominant — the 110 proved to be a superlative night fighter, with an outstanding array of firepower and two crewmen working together as a team.

Below: Another KG 40 aircraft, a 15 *Staffel* Ju 88C-6, rests on the ramp in France. This bomber unit was exceptional in using its aircraft against both land targets and shipping. The Ju 88C, developed as a *Schnellbomber*, ended up as an exceptional *Zerstörer* and night fighter with a massive forward fuselage into which could be fitted an extensive armament array, not to mention radar. KG 40 turned the solid gun-nosed C-6 into a fine anti-shipping strike aircraft, in much the same fashion as the RAF used the Mosquito and Beaufighter.

Opposite page, top: An all-black Do 217E from 9/KG 2 cruises over France in the winter of 1942—3. For most of its career on the Channel coast during that period, KG 2, along with II/KG 40, used 217Es to bomb England by night and to hit shipping in the North Sea by day. The versatile Dornier also became a night fighter since, like the Ju 88, it had an impressive nose for cramming in guns and radar.

Left: When Focke-Wulf rolled out its early pre-production Fw 190A-0s, like these at the Marienburg factory in mid-1941, the aircraft was still plagued with engine fires and technical problems. Nevertheless, the fighter was such a technological leap forward that it was released for combat evaluation with II/JG 26 in France. (*Karl R. Pawlas*)

Above: Egon Mayer's 7/JG 2 Fw 190A-3 'White 7' is serviced in France, 1942. From the start, the Fw 190 was considered a fighter pilot's dream. Light on the controls, with an excellent power-to-weight ratio, the aircraft was able to top 400 mph and was easily the finest in the world at the time, its only failing being that its performance diminished at higher altitudes. The Spitfire IX was the quick answer to the Fw 190, although Vickers-Supermarine did not intend for it to have such a long production history.

Left: A II/JG 2 Fw 190A-3 runs up at its base in France, 1942. When II/JG 26 had received the first Fw 190As in the summer of 1941 the BMW 801 engines caught fire or froze up so often that the engine and airframe manufacturers blamed each other for the problems. But when the RLM recommended cancelling the entire programme, the two firms were shocked into making some fifty co-operative modifications to the aircraft.

Opposite page, bottom: When JG 2 received their Fw 190s they were delighted. 'Red 1' of 5 *Staffel* runs up somewhere in France in November 1941. JG 26 had been the first *Jagdgeschwader* to completely re-equip with the 190, with JG 2 following suit. In spite of the fighter's sterling qualities, many high-scoring *Experten* refused to give up their trusty Me 109s. Having fought in one type of aircraft for so long, they knew each of its strengths and weaknesses, and felt that they would not do any better with something new.

Below: A common problem during the 190's early days, BMW engine fires almost ended its career. However, by 13 August 1942, when this 190 was having some serious trouble, most of the cooling problems had been sorted out. *Luftwaffe* fire fighters were experienced, effective, and usually on the spot in an emergency. (*George Petersen*)

As of 22 May 1942, some 65 British aircraft have fallen victim to the pilot of this Fw 190 on the Channel coast. With only a few exceptions, the greatest heights of German fighter pilot prowess were attained during this period. The *Blitzkrieg* in the West had ground to a halt, with the British tenaciously holding out and the Americans arriving to begin their strategic bombing campaign. While Hitler continued to believe he could bomb the United Kingdom into submission, and funnelled money and resources into bombers whose effectiveness was over, he let his fighter defences suffer. He could not believe that the last great war in the West would be the Defence of the Reich. (*George Petersen*)